D0743149

For my son, Misha

caper *n.* **1.** a playful skip or leap **2.** a high-spirited escapade **3.** cut a caper or capers a. to skip or jump playfully b. to act or behave playfully; frolic

One should not send
   a cat to deliver cream.

YIDDISH PROVERB

Cats sleep . . .

Anywhere, Any table,
Any chair, Top of piano,
Window-ledge, In the middle,
On the edge, Open drawer,
Empty shoe,
Anybody's lap will do,
Fitting in a cardboard box,
In the cupboard,
With the frocks—anywhere!
They don't care!
Cats sleep anywhere.

ELEANOR FARJEON

Set the cat among
the pigeons.

BRITISH SAYING

POLITICALLY CORRECT

cat

DEFINITIONS . . .

No. **1**

The cat is not fat;
    he is mass enhanced.

No.
2

The cat is not lazy;
he is motivationally challenged.

No.
3

The cat is not evil;
she is badness enhanced.

No.

4

The cat is not underfoot;
she is shepherding me
to the next destination,
—the food dish.

It's not a cat. It's . . .

A small, four-legged, fur-bearing
    extortionist.
A wildlife-control-expert
    impersonator.
A four-footed allergen.
A treat-seeking missile.

ANON

The Cats and the Birds

Hearing that the birds in an aviary were ill, a cat went to them and said that he was a physician, and would cure them if they would let him in.

"To what school of medicine do you belong?" asked the birds.

"I am a Miaulopathist," said the cat.

"Did you ever practice Gohomoeopathy?" the birds inquired, winking faintly.

The cat took the hint and his leave.

BASED ON A FABLE BY AESOP

My cat and I have an agreement: I leave her alone and don't make sudden moves when I wake up to find her perched on my chest, staring with an unblinking hostile gaze at my face, and in return she rarely mutilates me.

JAMES NICOLL

For a man to truly
     understand rejection,
he must first be
     ignored by a cat.

ANON

The kitten has a luxurious, Bohemian, unpuritanical nature. It eats six meals a day, plays furiously with a toy mouse and a piece of rope, and suddenly falls into a deep sleep whenever the fit takes it. It never feels the necessity to do anything to justify its existence; it does not want to be a good citizen; it has never heard of service. It knows that it is beautiful and delightful, and it considers that a sufficient contribution to the general good. And in return for its beauty and charm it expects fish, meat, and vegetables, a comfortable bed, a chair by the grate fire, and endless petting.

ROBERTSON DAVIES

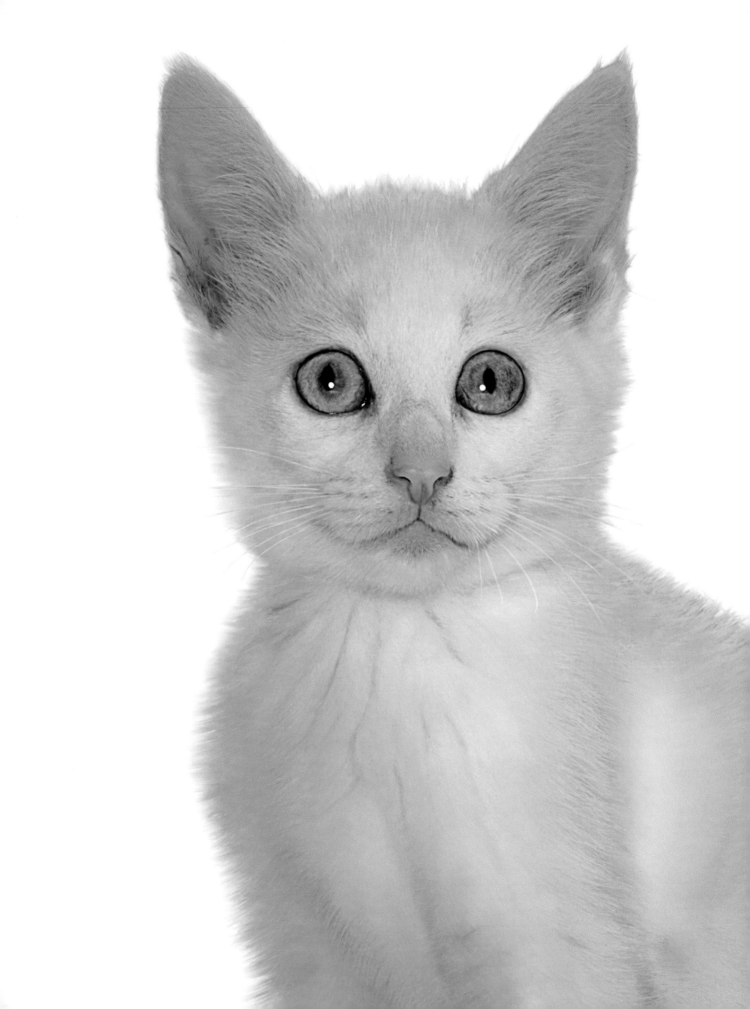

The black cat yawns,
Opens her jaws,
Stretches her legs,
And shows her claws.

Then she gets up,
And stands on four
Long stiff legs
And yawns some more.

She shows her sharp teeth,
She stretches her lip,
Her slice of a tongue
Turns up at the tip.

Lifting herself
On her delicate toes,
She arches her back
As high as it goes.

She lets herself down
With particular care,
And pads away
With her tail in the air.

MARY BRITTON MILLER

Dogs believe they are human.
Cats believe they are God.

ANON

Thousands of years ago,
cats were worshipped as gods.
Cats have never forgotten this.

ANON

Ode to a Cat

I think that I shall never see
A cat that sheds as much as thee.
Thy fur that sticks is all around
On chairs, on mats in little mounds.
I sweep the floor, you shed some more.
I wash the rug and you just shrug.
You should *give* thanks I tolerate that
Or you would be a crew-cut cat.

MAREA NEEDLE

Catch a tiger by the tail.

Fictional Cats

The Cheshire Cat appears in Lewis Carroll's classic tale, *Alice's Adventures in Wonderland*, which was published in 1865.

Felix the Cat was created by Otto Messmer, appearing for the first time in 1922 in *Felix Saves the Day*.

Tigger was first introduced as one of Winnie the Pooh's friends in *The House at Pooh Corner* by A.A. Milne, published in 1928. Tigger was based on one of Christopher Robin's (Milne's son) stuffed animals and is characterized by his orange and black stripes, beady eyes, springy tail, and bouncy personality. His catchphrase is "Bouncing is what Tiggers do best."

The Cat in the Hat is arguably the most well known of the Dr Seuss series of childrens books first published in 1957.

Sylvester the Cat was created by Friz Freleng in 1945 for the cartoon *Life with Feathers* where he first uttered those immortal words: "Thufferin' Thuccotash!" Mel Blanc supplied Sylvester's voice. In 1947, Sylvester was teamed for the first of many times with Tweety in a cartoon called *Tweetie Pie*.

Top Cat, the Hanna-Barbera cartoon series, premiered in 1961, and ran for thirty episodes, following the exploits of Top Cat (T.C. to his friends) and his pals: Benny, Brain, Choo Choo, Spook, and Fancy Fancy.

Catwoman, the feline villain/femme fatale to Bruce Wayne's Batman, has appeared in the comics, the campy 1960s TV show, and in the 1992 Tim Burton film *Batman Returns*, as well as the animated TV series, and the film *Catwoman*.

Let the cat out of the bag.

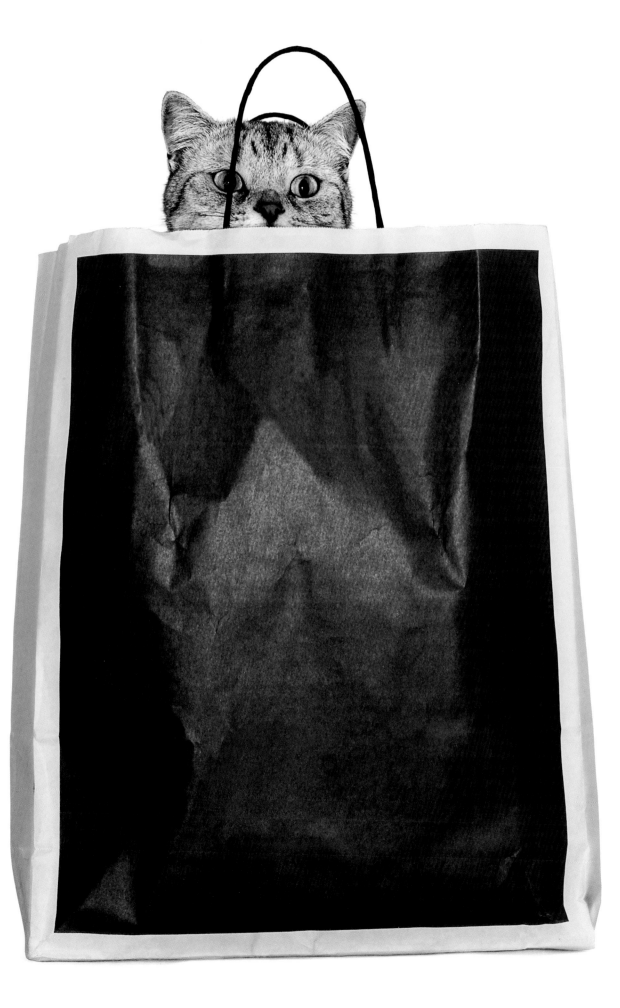

A
cat
always
lands
on
its
feet.

Siamese cats have a way of staring at you. Those who have walked in on the Queen cleaning her teeth will know the expression.

DOUGLAS ADAMS

After dark
all cats are leopards.

NATIVE AMERICAN (ZUNI) PROVERB

Catchy

Cats sleep fat and walk thin.
Cats, when they sleep, slump;
When they wake, pull in—
And where the plump's been
There's skin.
Cats walk thin.

Cats wait in a lump,
Jump in a streak.
Cats, when they jump, are sleek
As a grape slipping its skin—
They have technique.
Oh, cats don't creak.
They sneak.

Cats sleep fat.
They spread comfort beneath them
Like a good mat,
As if they picked the place
And then sat.
You walk around one
As if he were the City Hall
After that.

If male,
A cat is apt to sing upon a major scale:
This concert is for everybody, this
Is wholesale.
For a baton, he wields a tail.

(He is also found,
When happy, to resound
With an enclosed and private sound.)

A cat condenses.
He pulls in his tail to go under bridges,
And himself to go under fences.

Cats fit
In any size box or kit;
And if a large pumpkin grew under one,
He could arch over it.

When everyone else is just ready to go out,
The cat is just ready to come in.
He's not where he's been.
Cats sleep fat and walk thin.

ROSALIE MOORE

Cat Diary | *Day 752*

My captors continue to taunt me with bizarre little dangling objects. They dine lavishly on fresh meat, while I am forced to eat dry cereal. The only thing that keeps me going is the hope of escape, and the mild satisfaction I get from ruining the occasional piece of furniture. Tomorrow I may eat another houseplant.

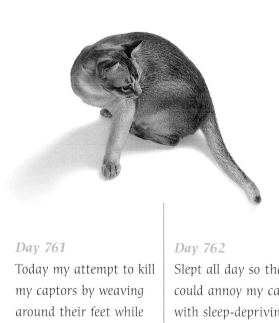

Day 761

Today my attempt to kill my captors by weaving around their feet while they were walking almost succeeded. Must try this at the top of the stairs.

Day 762

Slept all day so that I could annoy my captors with sleep-depriving incessant pleas for food at ungodly hours of the night.

Day 765

Decapitated a mouse and brought them the headless body, in attempt to make them aware of what I am capable of, and to try to strike fear into their hearts. They only cooed and condescended about what a good little cat I was . . . Hmmm. Not working according to plan . . .

Day 768

I am finally aware of how sadistic they are. For no good reason I was chosen for the water torture. This time however it included a burning foamy chemical called "shampoo." What sick minds could invent such a liquid? My only consolation is the piece of thumb still stuck between my teeth.

Day 771

There was some sort of gathering of their accomplices. I was placed in solitary throughout the event. However, I could hear the noise and smell the foul odour of the glass tubes they call "beer." More importantly I overheard that my confinement was due to MY power of "allergies." Must learn what this is and how to use it to my advantage.

Day 774

I am convinced the other captives are flunkies and maybe snitches. The dog is routinely released and seems more than happy to return. He is obviously a half-wit. The bird on the other hand has got to be an informant. He has mastered their frightful tongue (something akin to mole speak), and speaks with them regularly. I am certain he reports my every move. Due to his current placement in the metal room his safety is assured. But I can wait, it is only a matter of time.

Grin like a Cheshire cat.

I can't decide if I have a cat
or a cat has me.

ESTHER MARTON

Catapult

In a cat's eye, all
things belong to cats.

ENGLISH PROVERB

As every
cat owner
knows,
nobody owns
a cat.

ELLEN PERRY BERKELEY

CATBODYLANGUAGE

Tail

When a cat's tail is straight and tall, every-thing is fine. When it is at half-mast, something might be wrong. When a cats tail is dropped low, it means "I am very upset." When a cat twitches its tail back and forth, she is saying "Leave me alone." When only the tip twitches, she is trying to tell you she is self-conscious of her behavior. When it's bushy, she is mad!

CAT BODY LANGUAGE

Eyes

When a cat's eyes are wide open, it means "I'm listening." When a cats' eyes are half open, she is saying "I'm tired." Pupils in slits means she's alert. Bug-eyes means "I'm scared!" When a cat stares straight at you, she is challenging you.

CATBODYLANGUAGE

Ears

When a cat's ears are straight up, she is alert and ready to play. When her ears are flat and sideways, she is asking, "What's going on?" Ears downward is a warning: "I'm nervous. Be careful." Ears down and back is an alarm: "I'm angry!".

My Cat Likes to Hide in Boxes

My cat likes to hide in boxes.
The cat from France liked to sing and dance.
But MY cat likes to hide in boxes.

The cat from Spain flew an aeroplane.
The cat from France liked to sing and dance.
But MY cat likes to hide in boxes.

The cat from Norway got stuck in the doorway.
The cat from Spain flew an aeroplane.
The cat from France liked to sing and dance.
But MY cat likes to hide in boxes.

The cat from Greece joined the police.
The cat from Norway got stuck in the doorway.
The cat from Spain flew an aeroplane.
The cat from France liked to sing and dance.
But MY cat likes to hide in boxes.

The cat from Brazil caught a very bad chill.
The cat from Greece joined the police.
The cat from Norway got stuck in the doorway.
The cat from Spain flew an aeroplane.
The cat from France liked to sing and dance.
But MY cat likes to hide in boxes.

The cat from Berlin played the violin.
The cat from Brazil caught a very bad chill.
The cat from Greece joined the police.
The cat from Norway got stuck in the doorway.
The cat from Spain flew an aeroplane.
The cat from France liked to sing and dance.
But MY cat likes to hide in boxes.

The cat from Japan waved a big blue fan.
The cat from Berlin played the violin.
The cat from Brazil caught a very bad chill.
The cat from Greece joined the police.
The cat from Norway got stuck in the doorway.
The cat from Spain flew an aeroplane.
The cat from France liked to sing and dance.
But MY cat likes to hide in boxes.

Look at all these clever cats,
Cats from Spain, Brazil and France,
Cats from Greece, Japan and Norway,
Cats who sing and fly and dance...

BUT MY CAT LIKES TO HIDE IN BOXES.

EVE SUTTON

Way down deep, we're all motivated by the same urges. Cats have the courage to live by them.

JIM DAVIS

Caterwaul

Catsuit

FAMOUS

cat

OWNERS

(AND THEIR CATS)

Ernest Hemingway: *Author.* Hemingway owned thirty cats. His most unusual cat was a six-toed cat given to him by a ship's captain.

Sir Winston Churchill: *Prime Minister of England (1940-1945).* Sir Winston owned an orange tabby cat named **Jock**. He ommissioned a painting of Jock, who slept in his bed every night and was even taken to all the wartime cabinet meetings.

Sir Isaac Newton: Scientist and Philosopher. Newton, famous for his laws of motion and gravity, was a confirmed cat lover who was deeply concerned about the welfare of his feline friends. Therefore, so his research would go uninterrupted and his cats should not feel restricted, and be at liberty to wander freely in and out when the doors were closed, he invented the cat-flap.

Michel de Montaigne: *Author.* One of de Montaigne's famous quotes: "When I play with my cat, who knows whether she is not amusing herself with me more than I with her?".

Charles Dickens: *Author.* Dickens's cat, **Willamena**, produced a litter of kittens in his study. Dickens was determined not to keep the kittens, but he fell in love with one female kitten who was known as "**Master's Cat**". She kept him company in his study as he wrote, and when she wanted his attention she would snuff out his reading candle.

Dr Albert Schweitzer: *1952 Nobel Peace Prize Winner.* Schweitzer became ambidextrous because of his cat **Sizi**. When Sizi would fall asleep on his arm he began writing prescriptions with his other hand.

Edgar Allan Poe: Author. Poe used cats as symbols of the sinister in several of his stories, although he himself owned and loved cats. He used his tortoiseshell cat **Catarina** as the inspiration for his story "The Black Cat". Catarina was a house cat and during the winter of 1846 when Poe was destitute and his wife dying of tuberculosis, Catarina would curl up on the bed with the dying woman and provide warmth.

FAMOUSCATS

Scarlatti's Cat

One day the Italian composer Domenico Scarlatti's cat struck several notes on the keys of his harpsichord, one by one with its paws. Scarlatti proceeded to write *The Cat's Fugue*, a fugue for harpsichord in D minor.

FROM ISAAC ASIMOV'S *BOOK OF FACTS*

Dogs have owners,
cats have staff.

ANON

CAT CAPERS

Hamlet

Considered by *Guinness* to be "the world's most traveled cat", he flew nearly 400,000 miles after becoming stuck in a Canadian airplane for seven weeks.

Like a cat on a hot tin roof.

CAT CAPERS

Acoustic Kitty

In the late 1960's, the CIA developed a plan to obtain the Soviet Union's Cold War secrets by implanting bugging devices in a cat. "Acoustic Kitty" was trained to eavesdrop on secret conversations from windowsills and park benches.

Dogs are dogs,
    but cats are people.

Pussy-cat

What are vices?
Catching rats
And eating mices!

SPIKE MILLIGAN

Dogs come when they're called.
Cats take a message and get back to you.

MARY BLY

Catwalk

"Cats are less loyal than dogs, but more independent."

(This is code. It means: "Cats are smarter than dogs, but they hate people.") Many people love cats. From time to time, newspapers print stories about some elderly widow who died and left her entire estate, valued at $3,200,000, to her cat, Fluffkins. Cats read these stories, too, and are always plotting to get named as beneficiaries in their owners' wills. Did you ever wonder where your cat goes when it wanders off for several hours? It meets with other cats in estate-planning seminars.

I just thought you should know.

DAVE BARRY

A cat is more intelligent than people believe, and can be taught any crime.

MARK TWAIN

9 Lives

According to the common myth, cats have nine lives; in some cultures they have seven. This myth originated because cats are agile animals that can escape situations that would kill other animals. Also, because of an instinctual twisting reaction, a falling cat is able to twist around to land feet first.

MORE FAMOUS

cat

OWNERS

(AND THEIR CATS)

Jeremy Bentham:
Philosopher. Bentham was
so fond of his cat that he
had him knighted. Though
"**Sir John Langbourne**",
according to Bentham,
enjoyed seducing "light and
giddy young ladies of his
own race", when Sir John
matured Bentham had
another honour conferred
upon him: Doctor of
Divinity. "Great respect was
invariably shown his
reverence," Bentham's
biographer Sir John
Bowring wrote, "and it was
supposed that he was not
far off from a mitre."

Alexander Dumas: Author.
Dumas owned a cat called
Mysouff who was known
for his extrasensory
perception of time. Mysouff
could predict what time his
master would finish work,
even when his master was
working late.

Harriet Beecher Stowe:
Author. Beecher Stowe had
a large cat called **Calvin**.
He arrived on her doorstep
one day, moved in and took
over the household,
demanding food and
asserting his rights. Harriet
enjoyed his company and
Calvin often sat on her
shoulder as she wrote.

Raymond Chandler:
Author. Chandler's black
Persian cat **Taki** was his
"feline secretary" to whom
he always read the first
drafts of his murder
mysteries.

Calvin Coolidge: President
of the United States
(1923-1929). Coolidge's cat
Timmy would allow
Coolidge's canary to sleep
between his paws. Another
cat, **Tiger**, was a grey
striped stray adopted by
Coolidge. Coolidge used to
walk around the White
House with the cat draped
around his neck. When
Tiger went missing, Coolidge
went on the radio to appeal
for help finding him.

Cardinal Richelieu: French
Noble and Statesman. As a
kitten, Richelieu's cat
Perruque fell from the wig
(*perruque*) of an academic
named Racan.

Christopher Morley:
Author. In 1929 Morley
commemorated his thieving
cat **Taffy** in a poem entitled
"In Honour of Taffy Topaz".

Caroline Kennedy:
Daughter of John F. Kennedy.
When Kennedy's cat

Tom Kitten died in 1962,
the press gave him an
obituary notice.

Samuel Johnson: Author and
Lexicographer. Johnson would
go to town himself to buy
oysters for his cat **Hodge.**

Robert Southey: Poet.
Southey owned several cats.
Over the years, one in
particular, **Lord Nelson**,
went through the ranks of
lord, baron, viscount, and
earl for "Services Performed
Against the Rats". Another,
called **Rumpel**, had the full
title "**The Most Noble the
Archduke Rumpelstizchen**".
Others included **Marquis
Macbum**, **Earle
Tomemange**, **Baron
Raticide**, **Waowler**,
and **Skaratchi**.

Henry Wriothesley: Third
Earl of Southampton. After
Wriothesley was imprisoned
in the tower of London, his
cat **Trixie** allegedly found
him and stayed with him
there for the next two years.

FAMOUSCATS

Foss

Edward Lear was devoted to his tabby cat, Foss. His devotion was so great that when he decided to move to San Remo, Italy, he instructed his architect to design a replica of his old home in England so Foss would not be disturbed and suffer a minimum of distress after the move. Lear's drawings of his striped tabby cat are well known, especially those which accompany his rhyme "The Owl and the Pussycat". When Foss died, he was buried in Lear's Italian garden.

Scaredy cat.

CAT CAPERS

Lucky Kitty

Ivy Mabel Blackhurst, of
Beauchief, Sheffield, left
£20,000 to her cat Blackie.
For three years, until her death
in 1978 at the age of eighteen,
Blackie lived on in Mrs
Blackhurst's detached house,
waited on by a full-time
housekeeper.

FROM CATHERINE CAUFIELD'S *EMPEROR OF THE UNITED STATES AND OTHER MAGNIFICENT ECCENTRICS*

The cat's whiskers.

Concept © 2008 PQ Blackwell Limited
Images copyright © 2008 Gandee Vasan

This edition published by Andrews McMeel Publishing, LLC,
1130 Walnut Street, Kansas City, Missouri 64106
www.andrewsmcmeel.com.

ISBN-13: 9787-0-7407-7800-1
ISBN-10: 0-7407-7800-5
Library of Congress Control Number: 2008926400

Produced and originated by PQ Blackwell Limited
116 Symonds Street, Auckland, New Zealand
www.pqblackwell.com

Book design by Holly Camerlinck
Printed by Everbest Printing International Limited, China